Sukrita Paul Kumar, poet, and critic, was born and brought up in Kenya. She held the prestigious Aruna Asaf Ali Chair at Delhi University. Formerly a Fellow of the Indian Institute of Advanced Study, Shimla, Sukrita was an invited poet at the International Writing Programme, Iowa, USA, and Hong Kong Baptist University. Honorary faculty, Durrell Centre at Corfu, Greece, she has received many prestigious fellowships and residencies. Her recent collections of poems, amongst others, are *Country Drive, Dream Catcher, Untitled,* and *Poems Come Home* (with Hindustani translations by Gulzar). She is the Routledge Series editor (with Chandana Dutta) of "Writer in Context" Series. Her co-edited book on the eminent writer Krishna Sobti is the first in the series. Amongst her critical books are *Narrating Partition* and *Conversations on Modernism.* Her translations include *Nude,* a book of poems by Vishal Bhardwaj, and *Blind* (HarperCollins). A guest editor of journals such as *Manoa* (Hawaii) and *Muse India*, Sukrita has held exhibitions of her paintings. Many of her poems come out of her working experience with the homeless, the street children, and Tsunami victims.

VANISHING WORDS

poems

SUKRITA

Hawakal
PUBLISHERS

New Delhi | Calcutta

HAWAKAL
New Delhi | Calcutta

HAWAKAL PUBLISHERS
70 B/9 Amritpuri, East of Kailash, New Delhi 65
33/1/2 K B Sarani, Mall Road, Calcutta 80

Email info@hawakal.com
Website www.hawakal.com

Cover texture: Shutterstock

Paintings by Sukrita
Cover designed by Bitan Chakraborty

First edition January 2022

ISBN: 978-93-91431-39-6

Price: INR 450 | USD 13.99

to all those
who are struggling

to survive

the onslaught of
disease and the
loss of dear ones
in the recent times

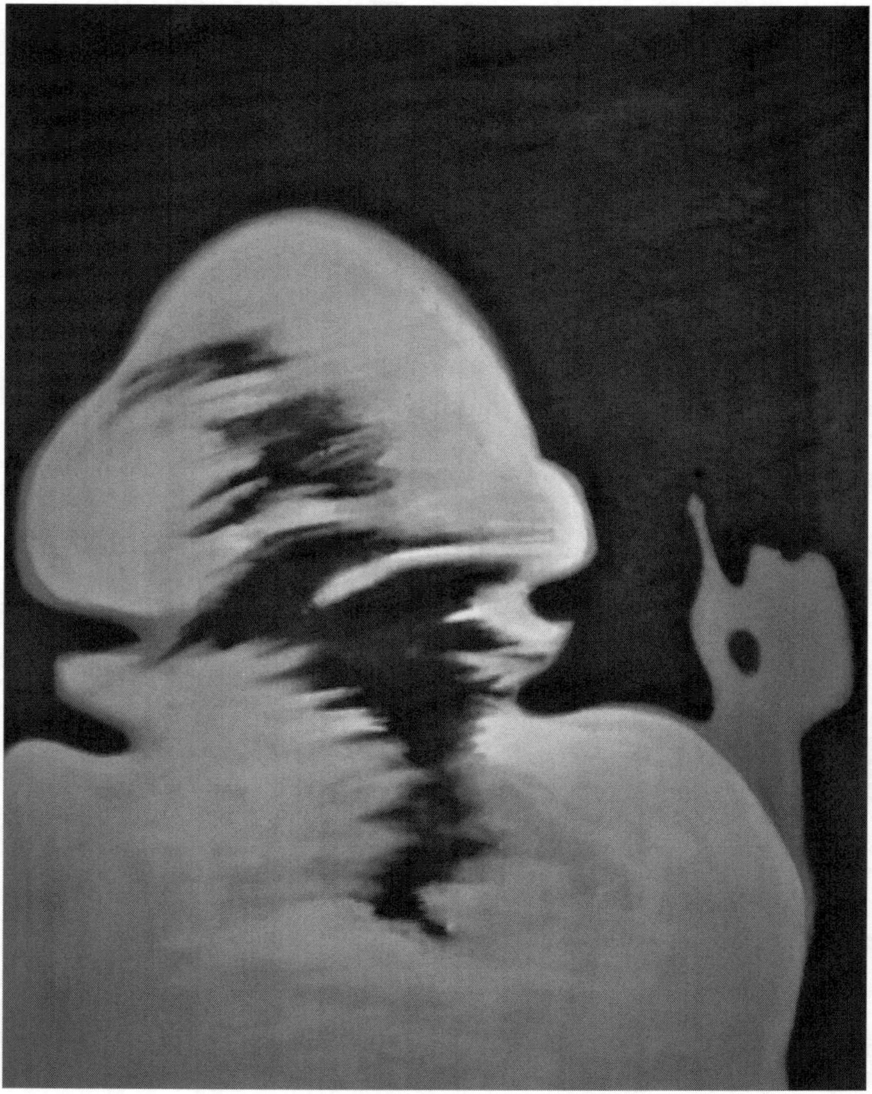

CONTENTS

On the Dal at Srinagar 11
Affirmation 12
Little Ones 13
Unwarranted Exit 17
Passing 19
One and All 21
Above the Ground 23
Alone 25
Memories 26
Pagoda Poems 29
Shaming Death 31
Animal Instincts 34
Freedom 35
Of Gaddi(s) and Goats 36
Good Morning 37
High and Low 39
Himalayan Tsunami 42
Painting Sunrise 43
Betrayed 44
Mountain Nights 46
Birthing 47
Card Game 49
Colour that Bleeds 51
Untitled 53
Kahani Ka Taana Baana 54
Naked Kailash 57
Game of Life 58
In Search of the Snow-Leopard 60
The Chosen One 62
Arrival at Paris 64
With my Chinar Again 66
Untitled 68
Cosmic Connections 69
Crows are our Ancestors 72

Why would the tiger of silence not leave
any pug marks behind in the forest of words?
My poems emerge while searching for these
pug marks amid the cacophony around,
picking words that cancel all noise in themselves,
such that pulsate in echoes of meaning and then
vanish into colourless space—
past sound beyond meaning.

ON THE DAL AT SRINAGAR

Drifting on the
surface of the lake,
my thoughts became
transparent.

For the first time
I saw my visage,
a cubist's work
of art
yellow, red, green,
blue and even bits of white
and purple,
joined together with
affection, love, attachments
likes and dislikes.

The boatman's oar splashed and
diffused the colours,
taking the muddle to
the shores in ripples and bubbles,

making my thoughts
once again
opaque and
dense.

Affirmation

I am not an etherised patient.
The moon whispers to me,

something might come out of
my nothingness
like

the complete circular wetness
out of
a bubble exploded

on a dry, blank state.

Little Ones

Time will not wait

for you

If you pause

to wind your watch.

✤

The newspaper reads well

when

nothing is happening

✤

It was a fatal accident

my mind encountered yours

some moments breathed their last

✤

Children play

with toys

adults with their

conscience.

✤

Unwarranted Exit

Gorakhpur

The black cloud of asphyxia
A live bomb
Settling on baby chests
Tiny lungs deflating
Squeezed of breath
Shrinking, greying
Choking and stifling

The fading squeaks
To each its own Hiroshima

The lactating breasts of mothers
Swelling in anguish, hardening
Boulders on their chests
Fathers sweating and fretting
in quest for God's plenty
in the air for one and all;

Comatose babies turn blue
One by one, more and more
Pale and blue

Numbers don't matter
Till they become razors
The edges rubbing into the heart
Sending shards of pain
And the tunnel to death widening
for the rising numbers to enter

Empty cots and hollow hearts
Fill the homes of Gorakhpur
Little ghosts enter homes abroad
Haunting the world afar

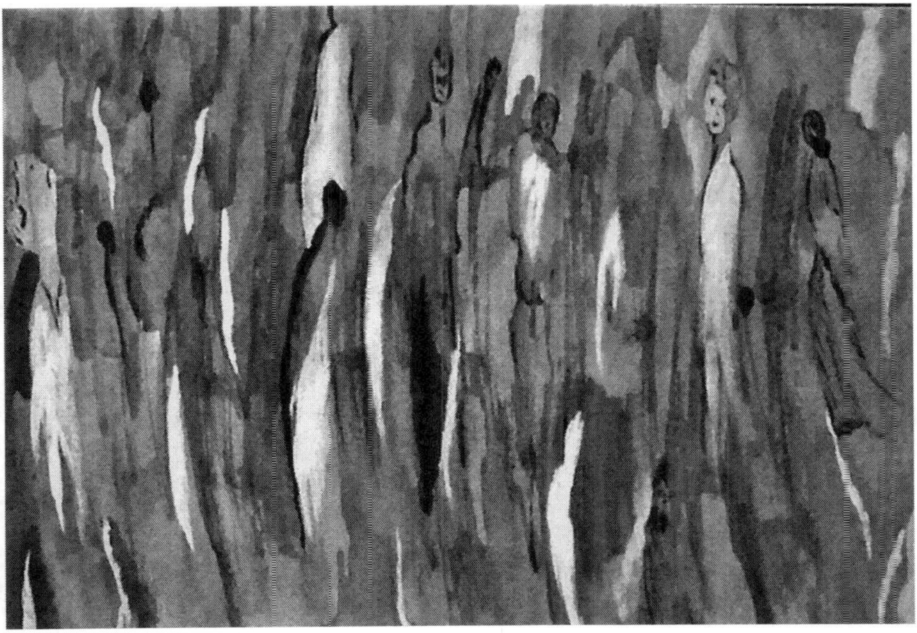

PASSING

As wordsmiths
They pulled and stretched
Sinews, nerves and muscles of
Words and letters
Idioms and metaphors

Shaping men and women
Carving emotions and ideas
in parallel worlds
story after story,

Narratives
Entering and homing
In many a mind

One after the other
They exited
Out of linear time

Holding their hands I grew up
leaping out of their laps,
Thoughts sculpted by them
Feelings borrowed, words parroted
All declared original

The air that rose from the
Leaves of those books
Filled my chest and belly
I lived in the creases of the paper
Savouring the new and the old

new worlds of wonder
in fresh language and gesture

revealing, not explaining
reflecting, not reasoning

In novel forms of being
ghosts arising from ashes,
sliding into bodies with hearts
and limbs taking them far

Those who created

They are passing away
Melting out of the icy words
Breath by breath
In search of worlds yet unknown
In the galaxies out there in space

One and All

A travel
Deep into time
Like it is now
I arrive at a space within,
Stretch a little to touch
That self eternally awake
Sharp and upright

While I could be amidst
Roasted potatoes
Grilled vegetables with
Bratislavian baked cheese
All inaccessible

Fish out of water
With messages of bon appétit
Rising from within
Butterflies aflutter in my belly

Stark white hunger with
Sharp teeth
Red tongue

I am hysterical
Who's there, the ghost
Or just me myself
On levels up and down
On land not my own

But then,
All humanity
Through centuries
Across all lands
The same hunger
The same pangs
Connect us all
When the distance between
Food and self
Is not covered.

ABOVE THE GROUND

Notes of Azaan
echo in the
twilight of dawn
as rays of
light enter
deep grey

Clouds half-sitting
on folded legs
for Namaaz
in the skies

Sparrows
perking out of
nightly slumber
shake their feathers
hop out of their nests
and swing along the
moon's slender curve,
chanting to the
fourteenth night
of the lunar month

Prayers lie in
unclosed parenthesis
suspended in the
firmament
This moment
This morning

ALONE

Can't there be flights
Into the clouds?

Will I always keep sinking

A rudderless boat in
Deep waters
Empty of colour

Waves folding above,
Around and beneath

Salty eyes
Sea taste in the mouth

That way
This way

MEMORIES

Your shriveled
Winter bark
Is a mere mask over
Those chirpy moments, tunnels of
Dense exchanges, breezy quarrels

Those hours of snow meditations

We soared through the skies
To the sounds of
The universe

The autumnal fall
cannot shed them all

Remember,
I am not the summer green of your
Leaves that comes teasing you
Again and yet again

On this wakeful
winter morning
I see it all

You are in fact
Empty of your ghost…
I see it all

Today too
Wrapped in that same
Green shawl
That ageless spirit
Emerges from the nowhere
Of tall keekers of
Jehanpanah,
Gently stepping

Through rows of shadowy trees

As on other mornings
Tiptoeing
Thief-like
In search for another form
An oak, a chinar or
Perhaps a peepal

The birds twitter
on my branches
As the mountains slide
into the jungles
on the plains.

PAGODA POEMS

Inspired by poems hanging over and around the *master pagoda* near Hanoi, Vietnam.

1.

nine times over
the word nothingness

emerges again
and yet again
in the twenty-word poem
by the master monk

the dragon, they say,
descends into the sea
searching for meaning
and spewing jewels
jewels that become rocks
with stalactites piercing into
bellies of rocks

columns of light rise
dressed in stunning colours

devils dancing

in step with gods

all in all,
adding to nothingness
and making meaning

2.

what is real?

image of the bird
fluttering in the sky
or the one still
in the gushing river

the wavy moon
in the water
or the one above
that is steady

parallel

forever

SHAMING DEATH

From time immemorial
human ashes are immersed
in the holy waters of Ganga
as phool, petals of divine flowers,
stripped of bodily apparel
streaming through unseen and
unknown water paths
Dissolving with the clay of the urn
Flowing with no destination
Entering the mythical and
Discarding the ordinary

Always wrapped in enchanting tales
of mythology and the sacred,
Ganga stands deeply shamed today
Disrobed and violated

Ganga rebels,
her chest heaving, gasping as
the bug infested human corpses
float in pristine waters
As unconsecrated bodies
Not sanctified by fire,

No burial nor cremation
The living abused by maladies
Death denied of reverence

Bodies are carcasses today
Dehumanized and disgraced
rolling wild over the waves
reversing into the world of beasts
Dispossessed of sacramentals
Divorced from rituals
and ceremonies
evolved over centuries
to respect life,
To lend dignity to death
as yet another journey

Animal Instincts

Elephants and Jarawas
Of Nicobar,
In tune with the song of creation
Heard the whispering earth
Felt her rumbling belly
Smelt death
And escaped into the
Heart of the forest
Away from tsunami,

Away from
the demon waves that
captured the civilized humanity
with their cameras
clicking pictures,
their televisions blasting
a hundred channels,
And virtual reality dancing on
their computer monitors.

FREEDOM

On the path
From nowhere
to anywhere

At the crossroads
When Buddha stood tall

Denying directions

What colours for the palette
Which notes from the accordion
Which words in a poem

Stillness total and absolute
When wheels at unseen speed
go beyond destinations

The spin arrives at a standstill
A foreboding perhaps a preparation
To start afresh
with no address

For the traveller to find and lose
herself
Yet again
On a journey of
no path nor goal

Of Gaddi(s) and Goats

Cackling goats and jostling sheep
Wiggle through woolly tracks
Reaching the edges of their skin
Rolling like pebbles down the Himalayan slopes
In herds

With several bleating little lambs
Peeping from the kukh of his apparel
The Gaddi's heavy feet
Drag many steps behind,
Hollering and bellowing, harking and heeding,
One arm waiving the threatening oak stick
At the sheep on the brink of cliffs,
The other cuddling the twitchy babies

My friend, doesn't the pashmina of your shawl
Whisper to you, tell you of the gentle strands of love
woven into the pashm fabric many times finer
than your fine hair
In its heat you may not cook eggs
Nor will its lightness give you wings
But what you wrap around yourself
Are the dense clouds trapped in the Arctic
Ready to rain on separation
Or melt into sprightly rivers in its warmth.

GOOD MORNING

Sharp and shrill
The ray of light enters the room
shearing the wavy curtains
knocking my eyelids open,
snapping me out of
the world nesting inside
so secure, so fragile
lying wrapped in
delicate covers of sleep

Inside, action in deep darkness
within the ball of time
with no creaks and splits
till light cuts through it

Eyes open to
cars galloping
on vacant glistening roads
children readying for school

the sun slanting over
black and grey heads
frowning under heavy baskets

filled with worries and nerves
battling with split time
doling out morning greetings
with heavy hearts

All over again
same motions of the day
from morning chores to
afternoon labour to
prescribed evening walks
of ten thousand steps
to a dinner of measured calories

Sinking into the couch
Once again I step into the world
behind the eyelids
deeper and deeper still
with all curtains drawn
into a world
Dark, secure and fragile

High and Low

Once again
That language
of silence
of dumbness

Bridges weighed
Under…

✤

Between the moon
And the sun

Like the earth
I am yet again
between

rising and setting

✤

Big wholesome moon
This month at dawn

looking the sun
In the eye

Defiant

✤

Himalayan Tsunami

The gaping holes in that old blanket
Spoke the language of deep sighs
Of hunger and deprivation

While the little head
Peeping out of the blanket
At one end —
— The head of Socrates himself —
Fixes a question mark

Lying across the gluey tar road
The norms of development
Running zigzag on the mountains
Through echoing ominous tunnels

To the town called Kedarnath
Where pilgrims turn ghosts
With holes in their eyes

Expressing their rock solid faith
Or the complete lack of it

PAINTING SUNRISE

Coal blackness mingling
with clear Prussian blue

carving depth around
the border
between the earth and the sky
the horizon

Slabs, one resting over the other

Silent rhythmic knocking

The wall crumbling
As the folds of colourful skirts
emerge, following
a long dancing foot

peeping through cracks and creeks

A thousand dark arms
embrace the rising bright colours

Betrayed

Beneath me
was that lush green grassland
Cushioned and calm
I floated amidst
Whiffs of cool breeze

When the creature with fangs
Dug its path out of the dark
centre of the earth

I watched that scorpion —
soundless and sturdy
Its curving pincers stiffened

in murderous focus
and complete alignment with
my fleshy toe submitting
to its sting
as though hypnotised

The sky fell over me
I lay crushed under

You had appeared
With love and pincers

Bringing pain and love
a flood of music

to drown into

Was that a suicide
A resurrection?

I weep that I have no tears
in the depth of my glass eyes

You whisper
When I am you
You are not I

I laugh with lips locked
Yes, I am stung
With the same thought
Moment after moment

Mountain Nights

I didn't know then
What I know now

The big thud on the roof
that cracked the rocky silence
of sleep day after day
was that of a flying fox
with wings that do not
carry its weight into the firmament
nor combat the mountain fog

Huddled out of dreams
I'd topple into the black tunnel
of night all alone
not in glory of the
moonlit snow
but in anguish of the lingering din
of sleepless nights

Treacherous journey uphill
difficult to climb
more difficult to come down

BIRTHING

On the gritty path
between nowhere and somewhere

and back again to nowhere

Buddha stood one-legged
Pinpricks and shingle
On the oblique crossroads
Where visible and invisible roads
Plummeted

Helmets and boots
Hands in white gloves, Buddha
Know-all of paths and tracks
Bequeaths no directions
The un-performing traffic cop

No colours to put on the palette
No notes to strike on the accordion;

Choices
Stretched between
logic and madness

When the mind is made up
Begins yet another journey
of torment
Gut wrenching pains in labour
Before the musical notes trigger
from the free metal reeds
folding bellows into silence
woolly cotton balls in thin air

Strokes of brush
On the blank canvas
Fill the void
With a rainbow that speaks
Of rain and sunshine
hand in hand

CARD GAME

it's a card game
they call it terrorism
the falling cards on the board are
screaming flags of victory

endgame on the screen
precision planning calculation
self and the other
all falling together

they call it
suicide bombing

gentle pressure on the button
placed in the hollow
of the belly
amidst the throbbing umbilicus
remnant of primal connection and
concealing legacies

of rainbows
of songs
of walking and talking dreams

wakefulness of a thousand lights
at the fall of cards
how many
          many gone

                    simultaneous extermination
                    a perfect unison in death
also a passport to life beyond

Colour That Bleeds

For Toni Morrison

Who knows when the earth was split into
Black and white
No record of any earthquake
Nor of any planetary catastrophe;

Is history lying buried in
unseen vaults under the seas
The ocean, Derek Walcott had said,
keeps turning blank pages
looking for history …
the one of lamentations

On diving into turbulent waves of the ocean
Peeks and darts of black history
hit and hurt

My daughter ashamed
Shoved into the vaults
Her blonde Barbie doll with bluest eyes

And in the real fictive world
The little baby brutally killed by mama

Comes back haunting in the pages of *Beloved*
Death saving her from return to slavery
Not liberating her from filial ties

What's not white is beauty wasted
It's just colour said she
to people not listening
But she writes for the black who do

White smoke and muscle
Pulling the cultural engine
White becoming whiter
Black, blacker
Between the two, an abysmal chasm
Filling once again with lusty calls
for supremacy at one end and
On the other
black screams and yelps
In search of their Africa

All held in the warp of time
Stained history petrified and written
In invisible ink raising its hood
Again and yet again

UNTITLED

Where shall I write
the paper twists in pain
all space is in awkward crinkles

Where shall I paint
The canvas fills
with sighs and whispers
As I lift those brushes

I carry the cross nailed by
Unborn poems, aborted paintings
Neither living
Nor dead

Kahani Ka Taana Baana

In fiction he said,
He lived a parallel life
moments became edifices
The writer constructed word-worlds
Away, not so away

Moments within moments
Behind and above each other
Characters
this one, and then another
Inner journeys and churnings
Mapping the outside
Building contexts

Sequencing time
Meaning woven
Across temporal borders

Walking up and
down the length of the room
one thousand times or more
The take-off triggered
And the story landed safely

On treacherous ground

One side used yellowing sheets of paper
Left-over blank sheets of an accounts register

His pen working on their chest
Drew out
The flattened sobs of the tree
Story after story
Tell-tales of a hundred crises

NAKED KAILASH

Betwixt Himalayan peaks
and human spirits
sometimes
masses of black shadows
and crows
lie trapped
in lingering pauses;

In the stillness
and the motion
of fluttering wings

waves of warmth
caress the slopes
and melt the snows
into cheerful apologies

for stripping the sages
the old mountains
wearing the
chilled privacy
of
white robes.

Game of Life

When I was born
my palm glowed with
pink fleshy pads
safe-guarding a deep long valley
throbbing its way from one end to the other

Now the palmist sees no life-line on it

It lies deeply buried under my skin
or perhaps its blown away with time

But perhaps I am not a corpse
I can hear the bird chirping

But maybe I am a corpse
I do not know why it's chirping

I don't want to burn
While being in fire

I wish to die
Since I wish to live

I will not let my palm betray me
I have shut its big mouth
With a line tattooed on it
I can hoodwink the palmist

In Search of the Snow-Leopard

To find the leopard,
Just follow its prey
Said he, his voice aquiver

Shadowing the prey
Fleeing in terror
Hatted and booted men
In search of Gyamo the snow-leopard
amidst white hills and vales of Ladakh

Binoculars cameras
Guns and knives

Vouching for what he had said
Shadows on snow emerged,
Of pug marks
In the white chill,

Dogs in fur coats
Barking in solidarity with
Guttural growling

Combating with
Echoes of chanting
from the monastery

Buddha rose from virgin whites
Filling the gap between
the predator and the prey
the seeker and the sought
Amidst
Cries of compassion and death

2.

Foot prints and pug marks
Are the remains
Of the epic tale
Of bygones
Marking a zero line in time

Foot prints and pug marks
signal a present
That has its feet dug
Into the past

Tornados come erasing

Foot prints and pug marks
Forebodings
of telling futures

No foot prints and no pug marks
Are proclamations of
Freedom from

Memory of targets
and victims
of revenge and guilt

The Chosen One

The monkeys of Summerhill
as if
motherless

No longer any chestnuts
For them
from this tree

This tree, the chosen one
Struck by lightning

The soul
as if
pulled out

One monsoon evening
The skies conspired
and fell on it

Life stilled
as if
In moments slithering

Brutal silence
Descending
Into twisted arms,
Embracing the tilting
seductive trunk

Roots in knots
The tree barren

Its silhouette in moonlight
Has monkeys on it

With chestnuts
as if
between their teeth.

Arrival at Paris

Many came, knocked at the door
And went away
But my friend,
Simone de Beauvoir
you didn't
You haven't left,

The Second Sex, Mandarines and all;
Pulling at the delicate membranes
of my brain, my self

Unknotting ritual from emotion
on the cross roads
of all paths
of my loves and my hates
you entered the doors and windows
of my inner scape

My guiding star, my lighthouse
My friend, you are my enemy
Let's face it
My arch enemy

Flinging me far
Out into the sea
Amidst sharks and whales
You led me to rivers of fire
Ismat, Annie Apa and Sylvia Plath,
Lal Ded and Maya Angelou too

All men, my meditations
For the birth of a ball of
Light and flames

My icon of worship,
The Greek Androgyny swinging
hand in hand
with Ardhnarishwar

Landing on this land, Paris
I see it all,
The ashes of lava
Over Simone's territory disperse
The fireballs of light darting
between the East and the West

Beyond gender,
Beyond the male and the female

WITH MY CHINAR AGAIN

O Chinar,
In some autumn, in some century in the past
When your leaves abandoned you
When all your colours merged into
the white of mountain snow
you and I
we got together...

Winter after winter did we travel
Seeds, saplings, roots
through strands of time,
strips of desert lands
From Kashmir of peace, of strife
Even through savannah grasslands of Africa

On the move...
homeland to homeland
Till we spread and reached
the paintings on the walls of Ajanta

In this life
when we were born anew
Partition after Partition

We remained in exile

In Africa … we met
Hush! Their majesties the lions
their golden manes
gathering near the pond,
jambo rafiki
They roar in one voice

Sounds rolling
into the lap of Mount Kenya
Chilled in its elegant white cap

O Chinar,
You change colours
Shed your leaves again, yet again
to be ready
for life after life,
death after death

UNTITLED

I see her now

Only when I close my eyes

On the screen that is dark

Illuminated by her appearance

✤

COSMIC CONNECTIONS

I am not the moon.
But I know I am.

I wax and I wane.
I am full and I also shrink to a zero.
I light up the night
and I convert the black to white,
and then to black again.

A complete turnaround to make it pitch dark.
A darkness in which glow-worms flash vigorously
to get their prey.

When I lose my dear ones,
they come over to my abode eventually.
Earlier I'd find my grandmother watching over me,
or sitting by my side.
Together we chomped peanuts in late evenings,
each nut popping out of its shell,
its crackle echoing in the universe.
Our intimate whispering filled the space with ghostly rings.
The rings floating in the Milky Way.

Then came my father through those smoky rings
Such that emitted when he smoked his cigarettes
Waiting for his beloved wife to pass through them

My mother arrived without any fanfare
Smiling, with her eyes twinkling
Alongside the blinking stars
No complaints no groans

All three generations heaving
Sighs of relief
In a cosmos full of
Intergenerational networks
Through shared memories

Crows are our Ancestors

I

At the congregation
of the black crows
under the foliage
of neem trees

Each crow
Stood his ground
And caw-cawed
The unanimous wish
to exit
the dark world of
Human aspirations

They declaimed loud
and clear
To take off into the
pink skies
To reach
the rising sun
To create
their own dreams

to live and let live

II

In today's congregation
Of the crows

The wise old head crow
Gave his resolute comments
Confronting the
Incessant cawing
of his audience
drowning the din
of the gregarious
jungle babblers

Come what may
Said he
We may lose our bodies
Feather by feather
The bill, neck, breast, wings
Legs and or the tail
In our resolve

If only to
Retain our spirit
Of mystery, of omen
of premonition and insight

And not be like the human species

III

I am a crow,
With the deep blue of skies in my eyes
The night is
Envious of
My iridescent black

But I seek that
Shimmer of moonlight
That lightens the density
Of black nights
And clears the passage
to the moon
beyond time and space

IV

Mountain crows are friendly
Just like humans and monkeys
on the mountains,

Not like the ones on the plains

Their caw-cawing knocks gently
On the ear drums

In sync with the song of the bulbul
Dissonant with the city-buzz

I hop on their wings and fly
Diving into the valleys

To Africa
To my Grandfather,
my hero
Who defied the
Suited-booted white man and
Refused to fasten the rails
with spikes
A century ago
He ran away
from the tracks

I have found him now
Free in the world of spirits
A crow amidst crows
in the mountains

V

No spirit in the body
No wind in the wings
The carcass lies in the centre

A hundred crows aflutter
Encircling lifeless feathers

Mourning death
They band together
As murder —
A signifier, not so
much to grieve, as to
hound the predators

Tricksters themselves, crows detect
Tricks in others

The dead they know may not be dead;
The living not live

VI

Pecking at his own shadow
On the glassy surface
The crow
We know is omnivorous,
Masochistic when hungry

VII

Crows here in America
Speak in a
Different language
One with a twang

Short staccato sounds
Ja ja ja, go go go
Even before you arrive

Back home, it is
Aow aow aow, come come
Lingering and melting
Holding you back
In moments of goodbyes

Come and go
Haltingly

both at once
in a world of contraries

VIII

Crows are not owls
Awake in the night and
Asleep in sunlight

Unlike owls, they are not
Sage-like and wise in one culture
Stupid and ullu in another

Anyone's home could be theirs
Anyone's food theirs too
Crows savour robin babies,
Hawks and eagles devour theirs

With humans their brains are wired up
They hate when hated
Love when loved, fear when feared
Crows have with us a deep
Linguistic and genetic connect

They are our ancestors